8 Lessons Every Podcaster Needs To Learn:
How To Stand Out From The Crowd With Your Podcast

By

Cheval John

8 Lessons Every Podcaster Needs To Learn: How To Stand Out From The Crowd With Your Podcast

© 2014 Cheval John

All rights reserve

No part of this publication may be reproduced, stored in a retrieved system or transmitted in any form or by any means, electronic, mechanical, photocopying, recording or otherwise without the prior written permission from Cheval John

ISBN-13: 978-1505506297
ISBN-10: 1505506298

Published by:
CreateSpace Independent Publishing Platform

Printed in the United States of America

Introduction

1st Lesson:
Start Locally

2nd Lesson:
Choose Your Niche

3rd Lesson:
Research, Research, Research

4th Lesson:
Send The Reminder A Day Before The Show

5th Lesson:
Be Yourself

6th Lesson:
Be A Good Listener

7th Lesson:
Send A Thank You E-mail

8th Lesson:
Network With Other Podcasters

Conclusion

Acknowledgments

Introduction

Podcasting has made a resurgence in the last 10 years.

It was a once forgotten medium because the technology was only available on computers.

After Apple created the iPod in 2005, many flocked back to podcasting because they believed that they could reach a wider audience.

There are signs that podcasting will continue to grow in the near future.

The reason is because Apple has led the way in innovation again with their new product, the Apple Carplay.

Carplay allows anyone to connect their iPhone to their cars.

It was released earlier this year on selected car models like Ferrari, Honda, and Hyundai and will be available on all newer models with the rest of the big name brands in 2015.

Even if you don't have the cash to spend on these newer model cars, you will have the opportunity to still get Carplay because Pioneer Electronics were one of the premier aftermarket manufacturers to collaborate with their new Firmware For Pioneer NEX In-Dash Receiver.

The product was released late last year and is available for any model type of cars.

One might think, This is all great, but what does all this have to do with podcasting?

The answer is everything, because the iPhone has given people the capability to download their favorite podcasts and listen to them anywhere.

That means that if you are small business owner, freelance writer, or a college student who is trying to showcase your expertise in order to land a dream job, etc., starting a podcast will allow you to reach your target audience and establish your credibility.

And it gets even better with Carplay because podcasters are able to reach people who have to commute to work on a weekly basis.

So you might still wonder, Why I should journey into podcasting when the medium is the 11th social media platform used by 6% of marketers, according to the 2014 industry report by Social Media Examiner?

The reason is because that same report has indicated that 21% of marketers are going to create their own podcasts this year and 24% are thinking of the possibility of having a podcast.

So if you are convinced and are ready to have your very own podcast, I salute you.

As you are thinking about what platform will best fit your podcasting needs, the third chapter, "Start A Podcast" in my first book, 8 Things You Need To Do Before Quitting Your Job explains what platform will work for the newbie podcaster.

When you come to a decision on which platform you feel comfortable with in creating your podcast, more questions will enter your mind like, How do I secure my first guest? Should I reach out to that A-Lister or should I start local with the people I know?

This book, 8 Lessons Every Podcaster Needs To Learn will be the step-by-step guide to grow your podcast the right way. It is based on the lessons I learned the hard way while hosting my very own online radio show/podcast, "What's The Word?" on BlogTalkRadio.

My hope is that you will avoid the same mistakes as a podcaster and that you will grow your personal brand and establish yourself as a thought leader, whether you are a business owner, freelance writer, college student or even an employee.

Let the lessons begin.

Websites:
Social Media Examiner:
www.socialmediaexaminer.com

AppleCarplay :
www.apple.com/ios/carplay/

Pioneer Electronics:
www.pioneerelectronics.com/CarPlay/

1st Lesson: Start Locally

When many people are first starting out, they are tempted to reach out to the most recognizable person out there.

The logic is that the recognizable guest will 'drive' many listeners to the show.

It is very reasonable if you want to start your podcasting journey on the right foot.

However, this is the wrong approach.

Many of these big name people will not even give you a second thought because you are not big enough, especially if you are just starting your podcast.

They will feel nervous because they do not know what to expect.

That is why it is important to start locally because your potential guest already knows you and trusts you.

If you built that relationship with the people who are prominent in your area, then it will be easier to approach them to be one of the 'first' guests on your new show.

And once your podcast gains traction, it will be easier to reach out to the 'big name' people because they will see your track record and, nine times out of ten, they will accept.

When I was in preparation to launch my show, "What's The Word?" I reached out to a 'prominent' person and she accepted the invitation.

Three days before the show was set to launch, she sent me a message saying that she was not able to do the show because she had to focus on her new clients and wished me luck.

Though I was bummed, it was a blessing in disguise because it allowed me to reach out to the people I already knew at my alma mater, Sam Houston State University.

The show launched a few weeks later and from that moment, I had many 'well-known' guests on the show.

So if you want to have a great start to your podcast career, it is really important to start locally.

2nd Lesson: Choose Your Niche

You might be wondering if you should aim for a general audience or go for a niche market.

You would think that it is easier to go after a general audience because you want to show that you are well rounded and also want to cater to everyone.

In a lot of ways, it might work if you want to display your experiences to a potential employer, or in the case of a freelancer, a client.

However, that can cause you to lose your audience because you are trying to please everyone and are stretching yourself thin.

The best thing to do when you are starting a podcast is to go for a niche market.

Whether it is marketing, sports, self-help, etc., you are solving a specific need and, in the process, creating a loyal following.

Dori DeCarlo, a seasoned entrepreneur, first got into podcasting after launching the show, "The Three Wise Girls" with co-hosts Debbie Barth and Linda Alexander.

During one of the shows, Dori did a two part segment on Mompreneurs, women who are moms and also entrepreneurs.

In the process of that segment, Dori found her niche.

With the encouragement from her co-hosts, Dori launched her own show called "Word of Mom" which evolved into the network, "Word of Mom Radio."

In the four years since launching, the network has received over 70,000 downloads in 2013 and is continuing to grow.

So if you want to grow your podcast, focus on a niche market because, in doing so, you will separate yourself from the crowd.

Website:
Word of Mom Radio:
www.wordofmomradio.com/

3rd Lesson: Research, Research, Research

So now you have landed your guest for your podcast and are counting down to the show.

One of the most important things you must do before the show is do your research.

You might say, "That is so obvious."

The sad reality is many people don't do their research on their guest.

The host might think they can 'wing it' with the guest on the show, however your audience can tell right away if you are on top of your game.

When you do your research on the guest, you will find out interesting things you never knew before, and from this research you can create some talking points which will be a guide for you once the show begins.

And when you ask your guests specific quotes, they will feel very valued because of the research you did before the episode.

Once that happens, the guest will refer your show to their friends who are also influential.

In addition, you will gain greater credibility with your listeners because they know that you are very disciplined in preparation and also your audience knows you value them.

Jared Easley, co-creator of the Podcasting Movement and author of the Amazon best-selling book,Podcasting Good To Great: How To Grow Your Audience Through Collaboration, grew his podcast, "Starving The Doubts" into a popular show.

His meticulous research on the guests before every show has made them feel at home.

As a result of his efforts, Jared's podcast has been named the No.1 emerging podcast by both Entrepreneur.com and the Huffington Post.

So if you want to gain more credibility with your podcast, you must research, research, research because, like Mr. Easley, you will earn respect from your guest and your audience.

Websites:
Jared Easley:
www.starvingthedoubts.com

Podcast Movement:
www.podcastmovement.com

Entrepreneur:
http://www.entrepreneur.com/article/237966

4th Lesson: Send The Reminder A Day Before The Show

I had booked a guest who was coming out with a new book.

Everything was scheduled and we were counting down to the day of the show.

Once the show began, the guest did not call in and I had to improvise while I was waiting for the person to dial the number for the show.

The guest sent me a message and said, "Her assistant did not send her the number to call into the show."

So I gave her the number and the show went on as usual.

I could have avoided the blunder if I had sent a reminder to the assistant the day before with the number to call.

You might think you do not need to send them or their representatives a reminder because they said they got it jot down in their calendar.

However, it is always important to send a reminder because it can determine if you will have a great show, a mediocre show or no show at all.

As in my case, the show was near perfect after the blunder.

So how do you send a reminder the day before the show begins without feeling like you are being rude?

Below is an example of how to send the reminder notice for your guest:

"Jane Doe, I hope you are having a great week and I can not wait for the show tomorrow. Just in case, here is the number to call five minutes before the show begins at 3 p.m. eastern, 2 p.m. central, 1 p.m. mountain, noon pacific: 1-888-888-8888.

Thank you again for taking the time out of your busy schedule to make an appearance on the show.

Have a great day."

Cheval John
Host, "Name of Podcast"

So to recap, if you want to make sure that you and your guest or the representative of the guest are on the same page, send a reminder the day before the show because you will avoid the awkward moment when you are by yourself doing the show without a guest.

5th Lesson: Be Yourself

Even though it is very important to have talking points from your research, you should not stick to the script.

You should try and be as conversational as possible with your guest and show your personality because a audience loves a person who is very authentic and willing to be real.

That does not mean you should talk about yourself the majority of the time while you are doing the show because it will come across as self-promotion.

Your main job is to showcase the guest and lift them up to your audience, not in the way that you do not have some disagreements about a particular subject.

If your guest ask you about your work, then you can chat about yourself for a bit.

Always keep in mind the 80/20 rule.

80% of the show is focused on the guest while 20% is focused on you.

6th Lesson: Be A Good Listener

One of the most important things a person can do during a podcast is listening carefully to what their guest are saying.

Most of the time, the interviewer will ask a question and then focus on what they are going to ask next.

When a person only focus on what they are going to ask instead of listening to their guest, they miss out on an answer so insightful that can benefit the listener.

If you don't listen, the guest will believe that you do not care about what they have to share with you and your audience.

When that happens, your podcast might suffer and it will be hard to build it back up again.

So if you want to gain insightful information during your podcast that will benefit your audience, be a good listener.

Your guest will appreciate it so much that they will give you praise when they are showcasing their appearance on your podcast.

7th Lesson: Send A Thank You E-mail

When you finish your show, the first thing you should do is send a thank you e-mail to either the guest or the representative of the guest who made it possible for your show to happen.

The reason is it shows proper etiquette to the person who worked behind the scenes to connect you to their client.

Another reason is the person might be connected to someone who you admire and want to have on the show.

Let's say you don't send the "thank you e-mail" or even a thank you note to the person, you might think you are not hurting anyone.

However, your guest will remember how you showed no appreciation for them taking the time out of their busy schedule to be on your show.

Secondly, the person will tell their friends about how you did not send them a thank you e-mail.

Once that happens, it will be hard for you to gain more guests because of the negative perception you have created because you did not send a thank you e-mail.

On the flip side, when you send the thank you note, your "guest" will speak well of you because they have seen you have taken the time to thank them for being on your show.

When you least expect it, the person will connect you to their clients that would make great guests for your show.

As a result, your podcast will go to the next level.

8th Lesson: Network With Other Podcasters

Networking is one of the most tried and true ways to get yourself out there and promote your show.

One way you can network is by commenting on your fellow podcasters shows.

If you do that on a consistent basis, they will take notice and it can lead to them promoting your podcast or even landing a guest appearance on their podcast.

One thing you must remember is that networking is about providing value to the other person and not just asking for something.

If you go to a networking event and only hand out promotional materials about your show, you are sending a message that you are not interested in building a friendship and that your work is more important than theirs.

You must go into any networking event with a giver's mentality and really be genuine about your fellow podcaster's work.

Once you establish the friendship, then they will be eager to help you to take your podcast to the next level.

The only question now is where do you meet your fellow podcasters?

The places you can network with your fellow podcasters is at conferences, online groups, etc.

One conference that comes to mind is the World Domination Summit (WDS), an annual conference held in Portland, Oregon.

WDS is the place where you can meet fellow bloggers and podcasters like Jaime Tardy, John Lee Dumas and Chris Ducker.

They have an established audience and always share what worked for them and how their strategies of growing an audience can work for you.

So if you want to grow your audience, network with your fellow podcasters because you will build your credibility as a thought leader and also lift up the people who are doing great things in the world.

Website:

World Domination Summit: www.worlddominationsummit.com

Additional Websites:

Podcaster's Hangout:
www.facebook.com/groups/podcastgroup/

Podcast South Florida:
www.facebook.com/groups/podcastsfl/

Podcast Community:
www.facebook.com/groups/PodcastCommunity/

The Podcasters' Hangout:
www.facebook.com/groups/podcastgroup/

Conclusion

You have reached the conclusion of this book.

Hopefully, you will apply these lessons in order to be successful as a podcaster.

This book can be applied to whatever work you are doing.

Whether you are in public relations, journalism, etc., you must establish trust with your clients, readers or your viewers if you are going to succeed.

Podcasting may not be for everyone because what works for one person may not be a good fit for another person.

The only way that you can know if podcasting is right for you is if you try it out for yourself.

If you decide to go a different route, these same lessons will be beneficial for you to succeed in the long run.

Happy podcasting.

Acknowledgments:

This book is dedicated to the podcasters who are successful with their podcasts and are serving the world with fresh content.

I want to thank Jared Easley for taking the risk in co-creating "Podcast Movement."

This bold initiative is bringing more recognition to podcasting and it can only get better from here.

Also, I want to thank Chelsea Krost because if not for her, I would not have started a podcast on BlogTalkRadio.

Her strong will and dedication is what will make the world a better place.

Last, but not least, I want to thank all of the guests who have taken the time out of their busy schedule to be on my show.

It is always an honor to learn from all of you and to share your stories of how you overcame obstacles to be successful.

www.ingramcontent.com/pod-product-compliance
Lightning Source LLC
Chambersburg PA
CBHW081759170526
45167CB00008B/3252